# English BASICS

FOR AGES 3-4 PRE-SCHOOL

## Contents

| | | | |
|---|---|---|---|
| Writing names | 3 | Words that rhyme | 18 |
| The alphabet | 4 | Learn about the letter n | 19 |
| Learn about the letter a | 5 | Learn about the letter o | 20 |
| Learn about the letter b | 6 | Learn about the letter p | 21 |
| Learn about the letter c | 7 | Learn about the letter q | 22 |
| Learn about the letter d | 8 | Learn about the letter r | 23 |
| Learn about the letter e | 9 | Learn about the letter s | 24 |
| Learn about the letter f | 10 | Learn about the letter t | 25 |
| Learn about the letter g | 11 | Learn about the letter u | 26 |
| Learn about the letter h | 12 | Learn about the letter v | 27 |
| Learn about the letter i | 13 | Learn about the letter w | 28 |
| Learn about the letter j | 14 | Learn about the letter x | 29 |
| Learn about the letter k | 15 | Learn about the letter y | 30 |
| Learn about the letter l | 16 | Learn about the letter z | 31 |
| Learn about the letter m | 17 | More words that rhyme | 32 |
| | | Answers | |

# Ways to help your child at home

## Introduction

Basic literacy in the early years involves *letters*, *sounds* and *words*. The following are some simple, everyday activities which you can do at home which will help your child's understanding in these areas.

## Activities to help with letter formation

These activities will help with your child's coordination generally:

- play threading activities with beads, buttons and laces
- make things with Play Doh
- do jigsaw puzzles
- play with construction toys (like Lego)
- try any cutting and sticking activities.

When helping your child write letter shapes, concentrate on lower case (small) letters and not capitals. Always encourage your child to begin each letter in the correct place and form the letter in the way shown in the book.

## Activities for teaching letter sounds

- play 'I Spy' using the letter sound (e.g. 'buh' not 'bee')
- have fun with sentences and rhymes where all the words begin with the same letter. (For example, say tongue twisters like 'Peter Piper picked a peck of pickled peppers'.)
- make some simple post boxes out of cereal packets
  - label each with a different letter
  - cut out pictures of things beginning with different letters and post them in the correct boxes
- have fun with rhyming. Think of a short word and encourage your child to think up other words that rhyme with it, for example, sun, bun, fun, run
- read lots of nursery rhymes together.

## Activities for teaching words

- make large name cards for the family, toys, pets etc. Give your child separate copies of them to match with the original set. Encourage your child to trace or copy them
- make labels for things in your house, e.g. the table, chair, television. Stick them on the appropriate object. Provide copies of them for matching
- make, and read together, simple captions under family photos in the photograph album
- take labels containing names of products from tins and packets when you go shopping
- look out for the same names in the supermarket. Encourage your child to help 'write' your shopping list with you.

# Writing names

## Look and learn
Everyone needs to know how to write their name.

My name is Jack.

My name is Jill.

## Practice
Copy these names.

| Ben | Emma | Sam |

 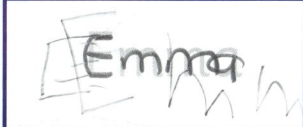 

## Challenge
Write your name on the labels. Join the labels to the toys.

# The alphabet

## Look and learn
Every **word** is made up of **letters**.

There are **26** letters in the **alphabet**.

## Practice
Join up the pairs of letters. Colour each pair.

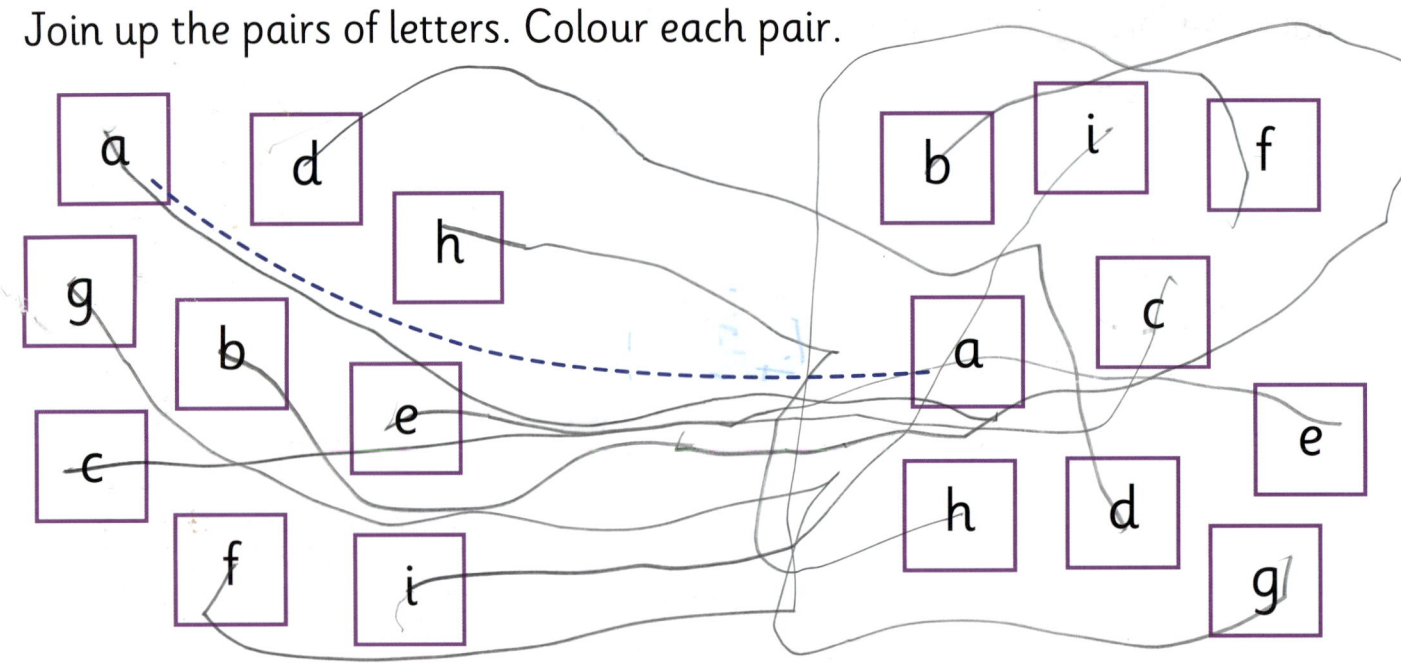

## Challenge
Fill in the missing letters.

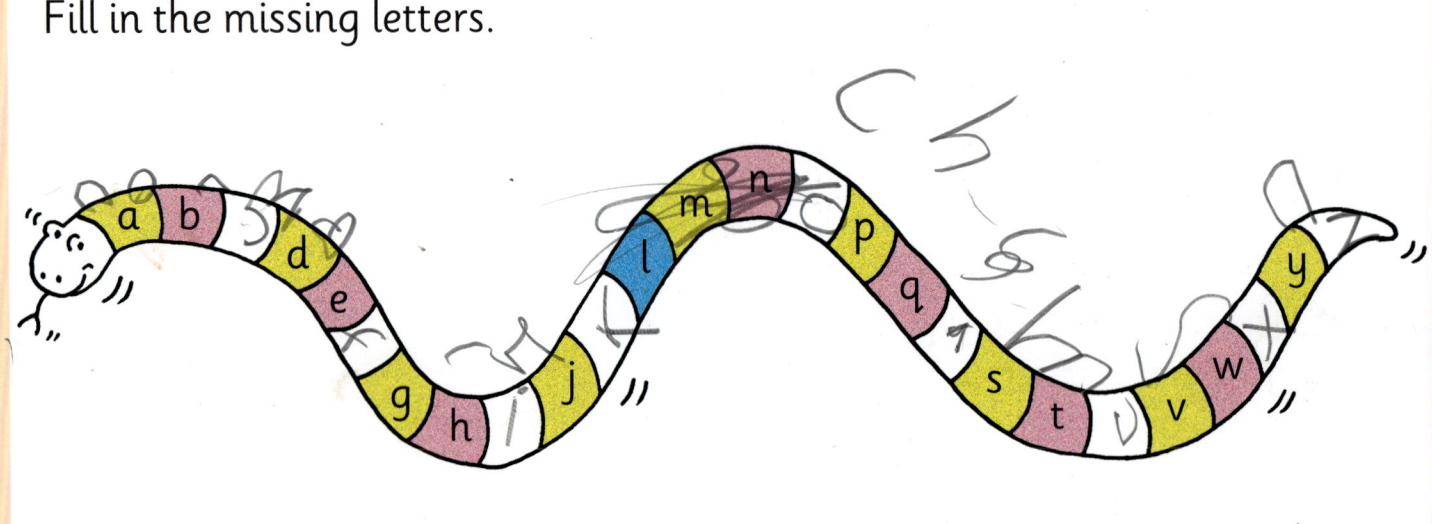

# Learn about the letter a

## Look and learn

Hear the sound.
apple

Trace the letter with your finger.

## Practice
Colour the five pictures that begin with **a**.

## Challenge
Find and colour the letter **a**.

Write the letter **a**.

Draw

an ant on an apple

# Learn about the letter b

## Look and learn

Hear the sound.

ball

Trace the letter with your finger.

## Practice

Colour the five pictures that begin with **b**.

## Challenge

Find and colour the letter **b**.

Write the letter **b**.

Draw

a big balloon

# Learn about the letter c

## Look and learn

Hear the sound.

cat

Trace the letter with your finger.

## Practice

Colour the five pictures that begin with **c**.

## Challenge

Find and colour the letter **c**.

| a | b | c | d | e | f | g | h | i |
| j | k | l | m | n | o | p | q |
| r | s | t | u | v | w | x | y | z |

Write the letter **c**.

Draw

a cat in a cap

# Learn about the letter d

## Look and learn

## Practice

Colour the five pictures that begin with **d**.

## Challenge

Find and colour the letter **d**.

Write the letter **d**.

Draw

a dangerous dinosaur

# Learn about the letter e

## Look and learn

"Hear the sound."

egg

"Trace the letter with your finger."

## Practice

Colour the three pictures that begin with **e**.

  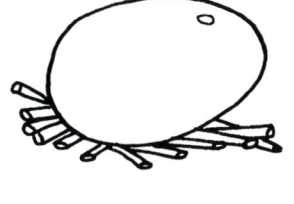

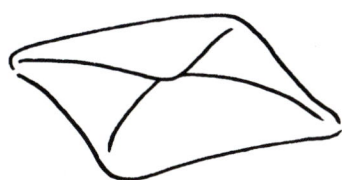 

## Challenge

Find and colour the letter **e**.

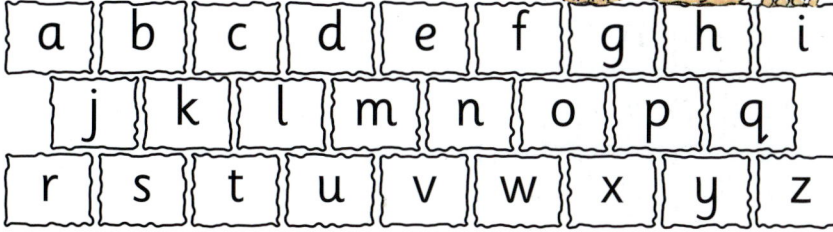

Draw

Write the letter **e**.

eight eggs

# Learn about the letter f

## Look and learn

Hear the sound.
fire

Trace the letter with your finger.

## Practice
Colour the five pictures that begin with **f**.

## Challenge
Find and colour the letter **f**.

| a | b | c | d | e | f | g | h | i |
|---|---|---|---|---|---|---|---|---|
| j | k | l | m | n | o | p | q | |
| r | s | t | u | v | w | x | y | z |

Write the letter **f**.

Draw

a fire in a forest

# Learn about the letter g

## Look and learn

Hear the sound.

**g**uitar

Trace the letter with your finger.

## Practice

Colour the five pictures that begin with **g**.

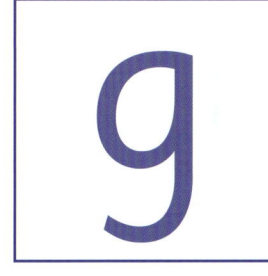

g

## Challenge

Find and colour the letter **g**.

Draw

Write the letter **g**.

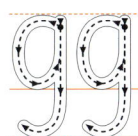

a green gate

11

# Learn about the letter *h*

## Look and learn

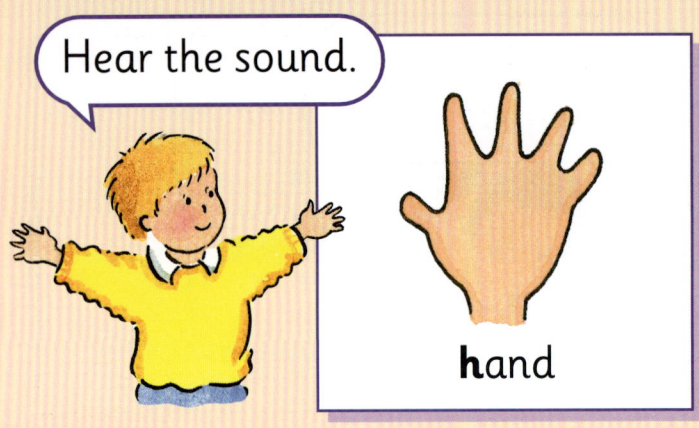

Hear the sound.

hand

Trace the letter with your finger.

## Practice

Colour the five pictures that begin with **h**.

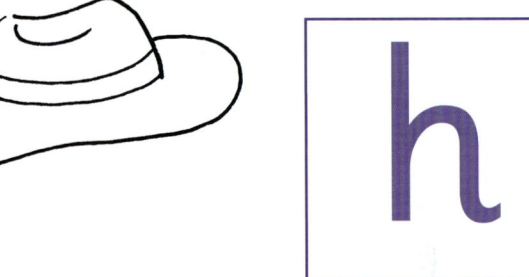

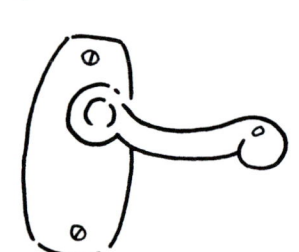

## Challenge

Find and colour the letter **h**.

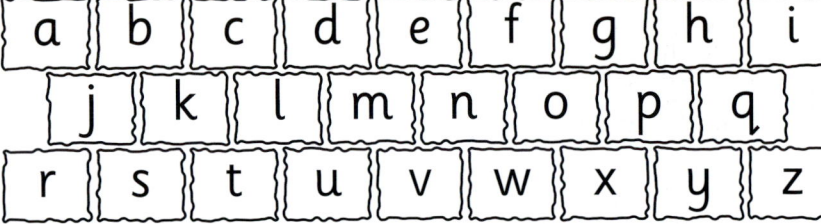

Write the letter **h**.

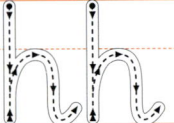

Draw

a high hill

# Learn about the letter *i*

## Look and learn

## Practice

Colour the five pictures that begin with **i**.

## Challenge

Find and colour the letter **i**.

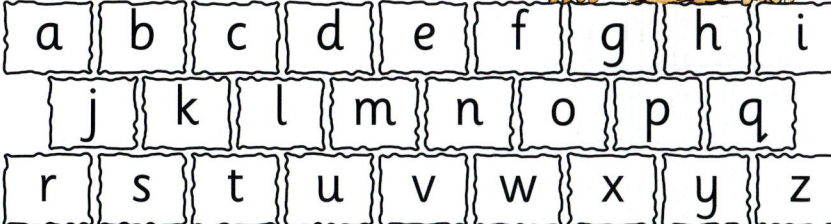

Write the letter **i**.

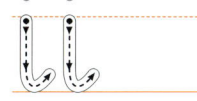

Draw

an insect going in an igloo

# Learn about the letter j

## Look and learn

Hear the sound.
jelly

Trace the letter with your finger.

## Practice

Colour the four pictures that begin with **j**.

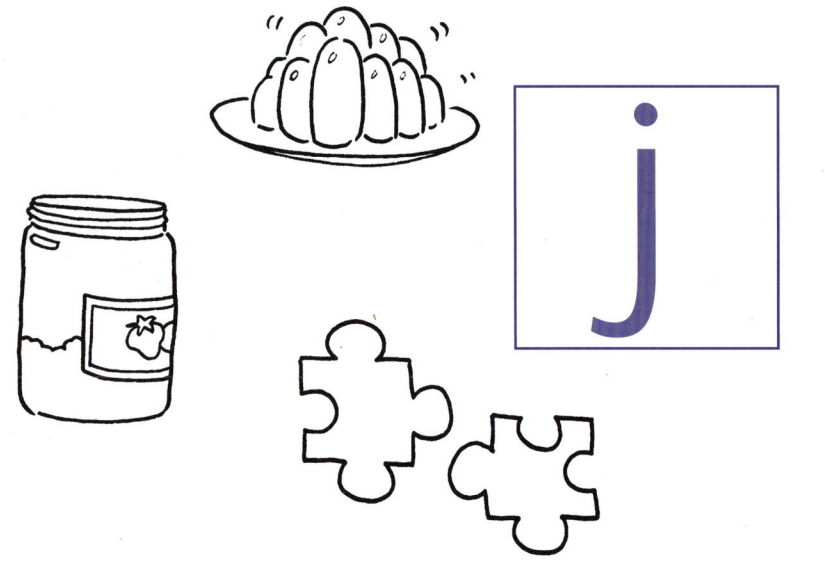

## Challenge

Find and colour the letter **j**.

Write the letter **j**.

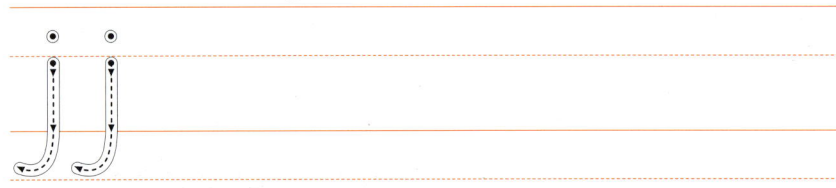

a jolly juggler

# Learn about the letter k

## Look and learn

Hear the sound.

**k**ey

Trace the letter with your finger.

## Practice

Colour the five pictures that begin with **k**.

## Challenge

Find and colour the letter **k**.

| a | b | c | d | e | f | g | h | i |
| j | k | l | m | n | o | p | q |
| r | s | t | u | v | w | x | y | z |

Draw

Write the letter **k**.

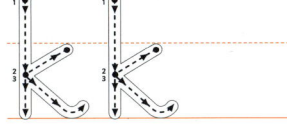

a kicking kangaroo

# Learn about the letter *l*

## Look and learn

Hear the sound.
lizard

Trace the letter with your finger.

## Practice
Colour the five pictures that begin with **l**.

## Challenge
Find and colour the letter **l**.

Write the letter **l**.

Draw

a long lorry

# Learn about the letter m

## Look and learn

Hear the sound.

milk

Trace the letter with your finger.

## Practice

Colour the five pictures that begin with **m**.

## Challenge

Find and colour the letter **m**.

| a | b | c | d | e | f | g | h | i |
|---|---|---|---|---|---|---|---|---|
| j | k | l | m | n | o | p | q | |
| r | s | t | u | v | w | x | y | z |

Write the letter **m**.

Draw

a mouse on a mat

# Words that rhyme

**Look and learn**

Say the words.

Hear the **rhyme**.   cat   hat   mat

**Practice**

Colour the two pictures that rhyme on each line.

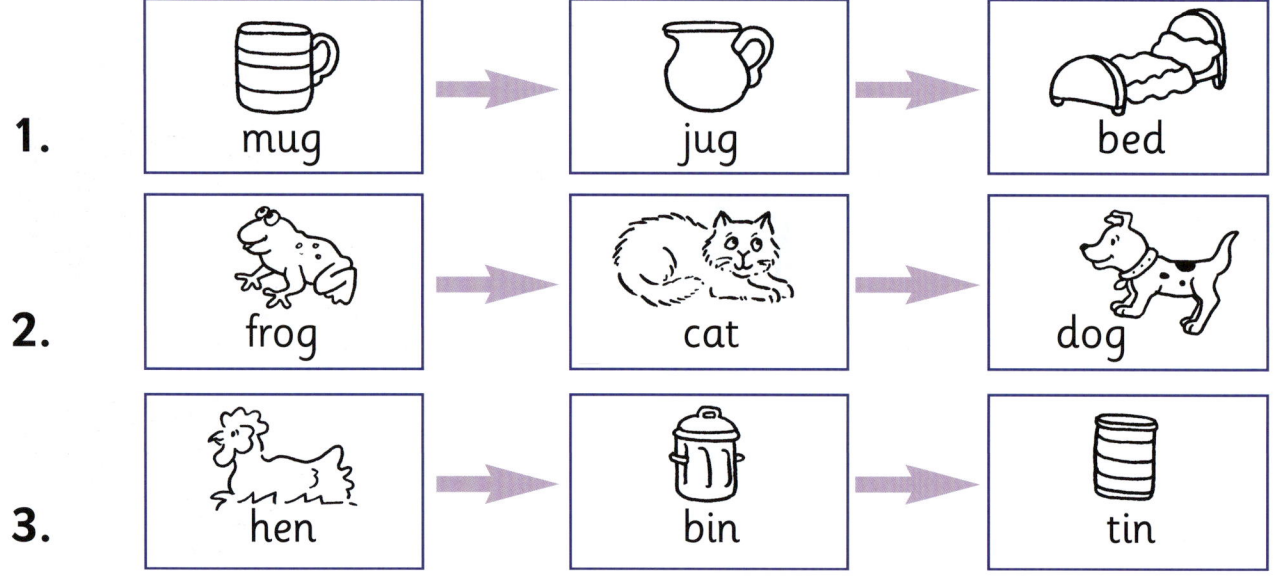

1. mug → jug → bed
2. frog → cat → dog
3. hen → bin → tin

**Challenge**

Draw

a hen with a pen | a fox in a box

# Learn about the letter n

## Look and learn

Hear the sound.

**n**eedle

Trace the letter with your finger.

## Practice

Colour the four pictures that begin with **n**.

## Challenge

Find and colour the letter **n**.

| a | b | c | d | e | f | g | h | i |
| j | k | l | m | n | o | p | q |
| r | s | t | u | v | w | x | y | z |

Draw

Write the letter **n**.

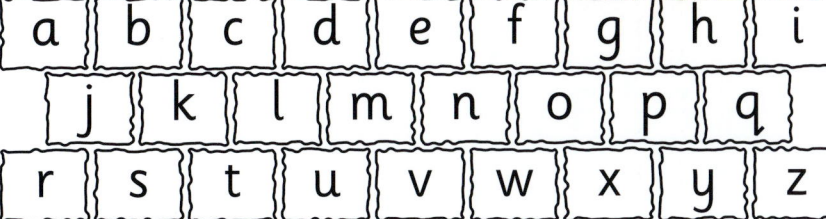

a new net

# Learn about the letter o

## Look and learn

Hear the sound.

ostrich

Trace the letter with your finger.

## Practice

Colour the four pictures that begin with **o**.

## Challenge

Find and colour the letter **o**.

| a | b | c | d | e | f | g | h | i |
| j | k | l | m | n | o | p | q |
| r | s | t | u | v | w | x | y | z |

Write the letter **o**.

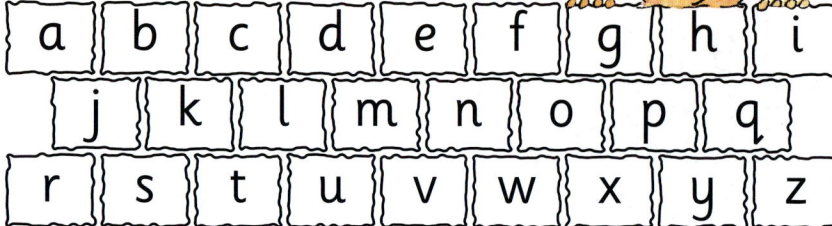

Draw

an orange octopus

# Learn about the letter p

## Look and learn

Hear the sound.

pirate

Trace the letter with your finger.

## Practice

Colour the five pictures that begin with **p**.

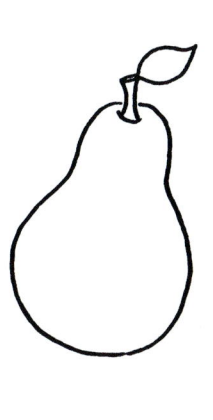

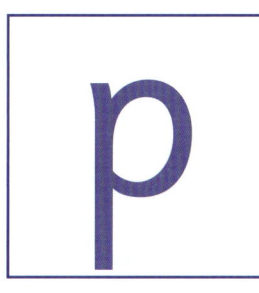

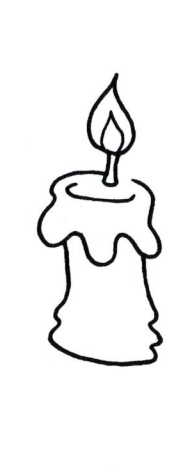

p

## Challenge

Find and colour the letter **p**.

| a | b | c | d | e | f | g | h | i |
|---|---|---|---|---|---|---|---|---|
|   | j | k | l | m | n | o | p | q |
| r | s | t | u | v | w | x | y | z |

Draw

Write the letter **p**.

a purple parrot

# Learn about the letter q

## Look and learn

Hear the sound.

quilt

Trace the letter with your finger.

## Practice

Colour the three pictures that begin with **q**.

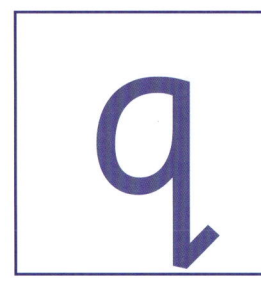

## Challenge

Find and colour the letter **q**.

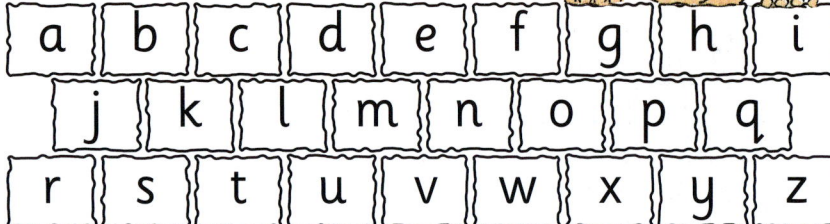

Draw

Write the letter **q**.

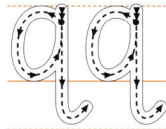

a queen under a quilt

# Learn about the letter r

## Look and learn

## Practice

Colour the five pictures that begin with **r**.

## Challenge

Find and colour the letter **r**.

Write the letter **r**.

Draw

a red rocket

# Learn about the letter s

## Look and learn

Hear the sound.
sun

Trace the letter with your finger.

## Practice
Colour the five pictures that begin with **s**.

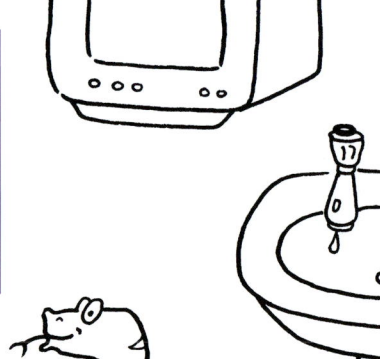

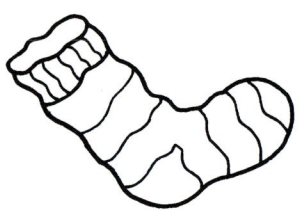

## Challenge
Find and colour the letter **s**.

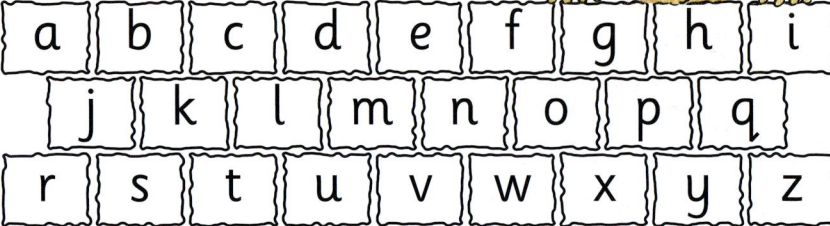

Draw

Write the letter **s**.

a sad sailor

# Learn about the letter t

## Look and learn

Hear the sound.

tortoise

Trace the letter with your finger.

## Practice

Colour the five pictures that begin with **t**.

## Challenge

Find and colour the letter **t**.

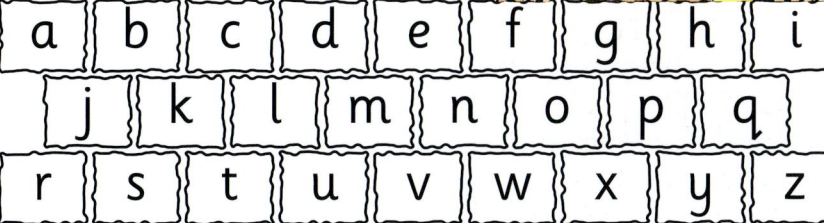

Write the letter **t**.

Draw

a tiger with a tie

# Learn about the letter u

## Look and learn

Hear the sound.

**u**mbrella

Trace the letter with your finger.

## Practice

Colour the three pictures that begin with **u**.

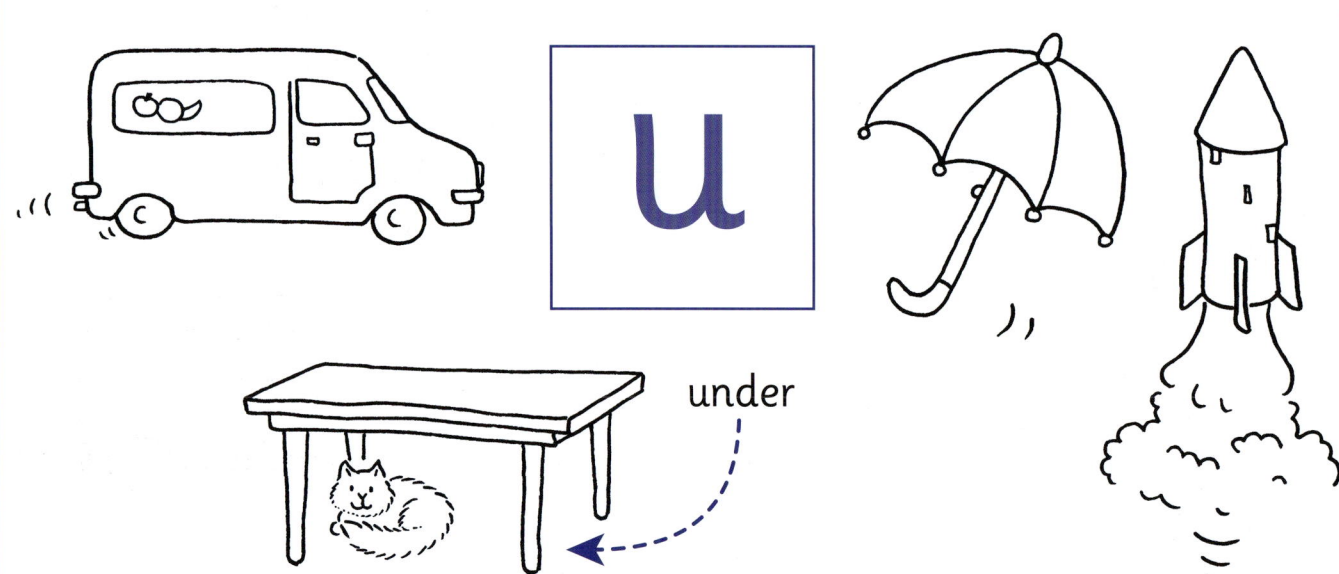

up

under

## Challenge

Find and colour the letter **u**.

| a | b | c | d | e | f | g | h | i |
|---|---|---|---|---|---|---|---|---|
| j | k | l | m | n | o | p | q |   |
| r | s | t | u | v | w | x | y | z |

Draw

Write the letter **u**.

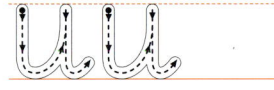

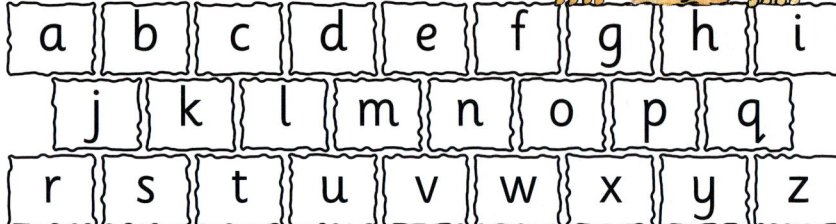

a girl under an umbrella

# Learn about the letter v

## Look and learn

Hear the sound.
violin

Trace the letter with your finger.

## Practice
Colour the five pictures that begin with **v**.

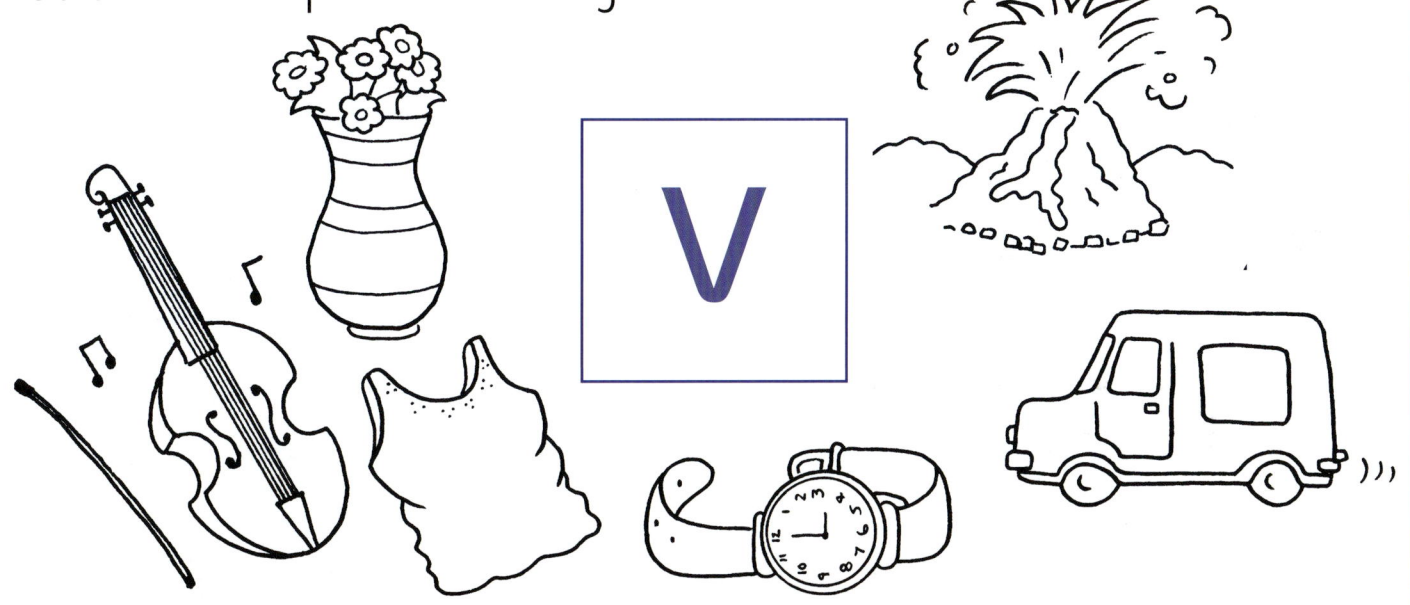

## Challenge
Find and colour the letter **v**.

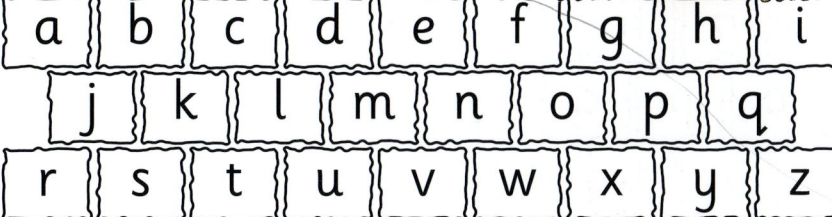

Write the letter **v**.

Draw

a valuable vase

# Learn about the letter w

**Look and learn**

Hear the sound.

web

Trace the letter with your finger.

**Practice**

Colour the five pictures that begin with **w**.

**Challenge**

Find and colour the letter **w**.

Draw

Write the letter **w**.

a wet worm

# Learn about the letter x

## Look and learn

Hear the sound.

fox

Trace the letter with your finger.

## Practice

Colour the three pictures that **end** with **x**.

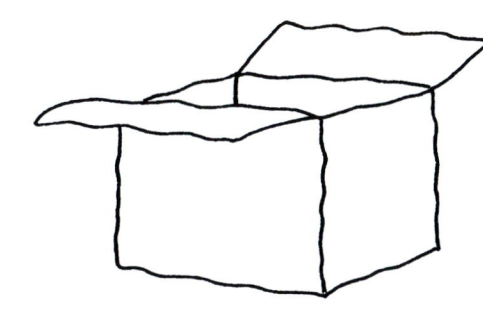

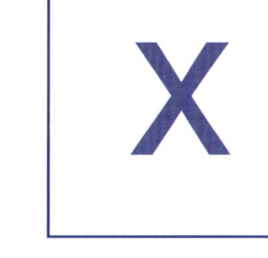

x

## Challenge

Find and colour the letter **x**.

Write the letter **x**.

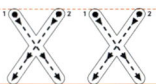

Draw

a fox in a box

29

# Learn about the letter y

**Look and learn**

Hear the sound.
yawn

Trace the letter with your finger.

**Practice**

Colour the three pictures that begin with **y**.

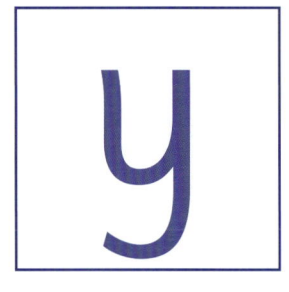

**Challenge**

Find and colour the letter **y**.

Write the letter **y**.

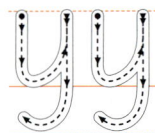

Draw

a yellow yo-yo

# Learn about the letter z

## Look and learn

Hear the sound.

zebra

Trace the letter with your finger.

## Practice

Colour the three pictures that begin with **z**.

z

## Challenge

Find and colour the letter **z**.

| a | b | c | d | e | f | g | h | i |
|---|---|---|---|---|---|---|---|---|
| j | k | l | m | n | o | p | q | |
| r | s | t | u | v | w | x | y | z |

Draw

a zebra in a zoo

Write the letter **z**.

# More words that rhyme

## Look and learn
Say the words.

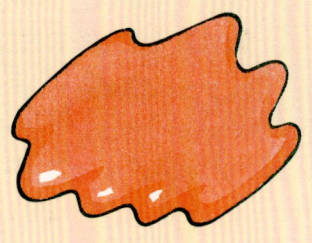  

Hear the **rhyme**.   r**ed**   b**ed**   t**ed**

## Practice
Finish the rhymes.

1.  a hat     a cat     a __hat__ on a __cat__

2.  a man     a can     a _____ with a _____

3.  a ball     a wall     a _____ on a _____

## Challenge
Draw

a pet in a net                    a frog on a log